Anne Hollander

Sex and Suits

edited with notes
by
Yoshiaki Shirai

SHOHAKUSHA
TOKYO

Sex and Suits by Anne L. Hollander
Copyright © 1994 by Anne Hollander
Japanese translation published by arrangement with
Alfred A Knopf, Inc. through The English Agency
(Japan)Ltd.

はしがき

　近代スーツの原型が誕生したのは17世紀後半で，その後幾多の改良が加えられ，19世紀中頃には現在見られるような型が確立されたといわれている。スーツはこれまでの長いあいだ，男性に最も相応しい衣服として着用されてきた。今後もその傾向は続くと思われる。ところが，あまりにも一般的になりすぎたためにスーツは標準的な紳士服となり，そのために，これをファッションと見なすことはほとんどなかった。しかし，ニューヨーク人文科学研究所特別研究員で，美術史家のアン・ホランダーは違う見方をする。彼女によれば，スーツは男性の自尊心を十二分に視覚化したものであり，機能的でありながら「高潔と抑制，思慮分別と公平」を象徴するすぐれた「芸術作品」であり，スーツこそが女性のファッションの根源であるという。それに対して女性服はドレスのバリエーションを作る以外ファッションの発展になんら貢献せず，単に男性服の模倣としての「新しさ」しか導入しなかった，と彼女は主張する。

　本書はそうした内容を持つ *Sex and Suits: The Evolution of Modern Dress* (1994) から，ホランダーが彼女自身のテーマを概略していると思われる部分を抜粋したものである。そこではセクシュアリティといった性の問題が服装史とからめて論じられており，当然ながらそこからは西洋社会における男性と女性の役割の違いについて，といった文化論も展開される。このように，本書でとりあげた部分は単なる皮相的な服装史の概略に終わっていない。西洋文化についての洞察が，本書での英語学習をとおしてさらに深化するのであれば望外の幸せである。

　著者ホランダーには，ほかに *Seeing Through Clothes* (1978) と *Moving*

Pictures (1989) の著書がある。彼女は現在，ニューヨークとパリの両市に交互に住んでいるとのことである。

　本書の注をつけるにあたっては，学習の便を考慮してできるだけ詳しくするように心がけた。

白井義昭

Contents

はしがき ……………………………………………………… i
1. Form and Sexuality ……………………………………… 1
2. Early Fashion History ………………………………… 16
3. Later Changes …………………………………………… 31
4. Female Invention ……………………………………… 41
   Notes …………………………………………………… 51

1. Form and Sexuality

Modern Desire is subversive. Modern fashion, acting as the illustrator of modern civilization's discontents, never tries to tame collective fantasy into a fixed shape meant to last, but is always prodding it, urging it to keep on making awkward new suggestions instead of repeating fine old assertions. In literary fictions, modern need moves away from the comfort of repetitive incantation and saga toward compact lyric and the phrasing of vivid and disturbing personal narrative; and the same applies in the visual domain.

Whenever the chief desire of the eye is a reliance on immemorial forms, the prevailing esthetic spirit isn't modern. For visual satisfaction, modernity requires conflict and dialectic, uneasy combination, ambiguity and tension, irony, the look of dissatisfied search. This means that any clear and stable modern visual harmony, if and when it is achieved, depends on tension and sacrifice, the posture of imaginative vigilance —you can see it in the best works of abstract painting or sculpture and in modern architecture, and you can see it in modern abstract suits. When rightly managed, such balanced and coherent simplicity always looks vibrant and not dull, never static but always charged with potential change — and indeed sexy. Modern simplicity has become one highly erotic theme at play in all forms of design.

For modern clothes, sexuality became the fundamental expressive motor, the underlying source of creative play, of waywardness, of invention including both the practical and the regressive kind: fashion came to portray sexuality itself as lawless, wayward and inventive. All indices of social class and function were contained by the sexual mode, so that men's clothes were always noticeably masculine first, and only afterwards noble, professional, rural, proletarian. Since fashion started, the forms that expounded the male or female body in dress were generated by sexual fantasy and then tempered to suit other dimensions of life. I would emphasize that *sexuality*, which I claim as the foundation for form in fashion, is not the same thing as *seductiveness*. This last has emerged and subsided in fashion for either sex at certain periods; but I would claim that sexuality itself is behind any strong form in fashion whether or not the form calls attention to the sexual characteristics of the wearer. Sexuality, that is, as distinct from any simple differentiation between male and female.

All this only became true when Western fashion got fully under way, somewhere between 1200 and 1400. Elegant clothes during that period, after consisting of the same basic shapes on which ornament provided the interest, began to require padding or constriction for the torso, extreme shortness or trailing length for garments, and carefully wrought, expressive shapes for shoes, sleeves, and headgear — and to keep changing these requirements. There was a new insistence on cut and fit, to shape the torso tightly and sometimes strangely, and then to change the shape. The same period saw a new use of extra fabric to extend the body's visual scope, to create conspicuous and kinetic shapes around it that obviously went against the force of practical need, and well beyond a social need for simple ostentation. Eventually parts of the body might be smoothly packed away, but then referred to on the surface. A woman's bodice, for example, instead of allowing her breasts to form hills under the fabric, would be made to flatten out all her fleshly curves into an abstract cone, which would then be adorned with two semicircular festoons of pearls. These would replace the natural curves of the breasts with a reference suggesting that breasts themselves are ornaments.

This very fashion, originating in sixteenth-century France but apparent at other European courts, is a good example of how pictorial fashion had already become by that time. The style is now known only from painted and engraved portraits, like so many other modes; and it was also undoubtedly promulgated among the noble ladies of Europe by engravings and miniatures in its own time. Only artists could make a bodice so smooth, the chest above so uniformly waxen, shoulders so boneless, and pearls so perfectly draped. Life was undoubtedly already imitating art in the sixteenth century, and the fashion seems to be referring to pictorial conventions stricter than itself. But its power to satisfy lay deeper than that, in the new representational force of fashion, which allowed a retreat from the actuality of breasts into the abstract, emblematic figure dress could make them a part of.

It was with the development of such devices in fashion that dress became a modern art. It began to operate symbolically and allusively through fashionable shape and ornament, using its own suggestive applied forms in a dynamic counterpoint to the shapes of real bodies. Fashion has done this ever since, just as art has done, making its own agreement with natural forms to create a vital sequence in its own medium. But in fashion, of course, part of the medium is always the live person experiencing its life.

In harmony with the other visual arts at the same time, clothing came to propose a three-dimensional and illusionistic program for the clothed body, a new fictional medium, a poetic form, something that conveyed imagined truths with the added status of reported facts, a drama using live actors. The body itself became fictionalized. Persons became figures and characters, not just members of groups. Fashion invented a poetic visual vocabulary to demonstrate, even unconsciously, overlapping and simultaneous themes of temporality and contingency, or social placement and personality, but always cast in the terms of sexuality that are demanded by the living body, hers or his. Competitive dressing came to be based on suggestive changes in shape, color, line and proportion, all with respect to bodily shapes, and on variable piquancy in the forms of ornaments, not just on their value.

As a part of the drama of sexuality, the fiction of fashion began to deal with the idea of phrasing through time, adroitly joining the forces of memory and desire in one picture, framed by awareness of death. The desirable visual mode came to depend on a peculiar difference between a present way to look and an earlier way, not just between silk and homespun, nor between sleek and crude adornment, nor between different symbolic colors, nor even simply between this way and that way of wrapping the same sash. A sense of dramatic sequence, rather than of static apparition, came to underlie the quality of desirable appearance. Rich and poor effects kept their obvious significance, but the representational medium of fashion came to impose its own construction on them, editing any direct meaning they carried. Crudity might be temporarily witty, refinement tacky; and past effects were always to be recycled in new contexts to make detached comment on former taste.

Beauty ceased to be an acknowledged aim of fashion, as it remains in so many non-modern, traditional arts. Beauty in fashion comes always as a sort of vivid surprise, as it often does in the experience of sexual love. In fashion, beauty doesn't result from the confident harmony of known form and material, but from brilliant moments of clarified vision. Such moments may be born of desire, but they are always sustained in art, as I suggested earlier, by vigilance, technique and imagination. Above all, beauty in fashion is constantly created *ad hoc* by the pictorial artists who make a medium for it and convey it everywhere, who can make the beauty of an image seem identical with the beauty of a garment.

Insisting further on the theme of sex, men and women began to dress extremely differently from each other somewhere during the fourteenth century, having worked up to it rather slowly during the two before. After that, the borrowing of visual motifs across a visually sharper sexual divide created more suggestive interest and emotional tension in clothing than it ever could have done when men and women wore similarly designed garments. Small suggestions of transvestism became more noticeable and more exciting.

Art shows how the change worked. In the early Middle Ages until about 1100, when garments for both sexes were still relatively shapeless, relief sculptures and mosaics tended to create one unifying pattern of drapery inside compositions that combined male and female figures. The result was that the clothing seemed to link the sexes instead of dividing them. This scheme for clothes in art derived partly from such Classical monuments as the celebrated *Ara Pacis* of the Emperor Augustus from the early first century B.C., where the frieze of men and women is awash in a rhythmic arrangement of drapery.

This particular Roman drapery seems to clothe everybody

1. Form and Sexuality 7

ABOVE: Roman bas-relief, *Ara Pacis*, west elevation, Rome, 13-9 B.C. BELOW: Byzantine mosaic, *The Empress Theodora and Retinue*, Ravenna, 500-526 A.D.

Although male and female clothes actually differed, the artists of antiquity and the early Middle Ages showed men and women similarly draped and of similar size and shape. All clothing has been uniformly stylized so as to unite rather than separate the two sexes.

ABOVE: Manuscript illumination, *Le Roman de la violette*, French, mid-fifteenth century. LEFT: Master E.S., engraving, *The Knight and His Lady*, German, mid-fifteenth century.

Vivid new differences between male and female dress characterize the first developments of true fashion, and are emphasized by the artists of the late Middle Ages and the early Renaissance. Male fashion is based on the brilliant bodily articulations of plate armor (left), while female fashion exaggerates the enveloping skirt below with a very small tight bodice above. Men now have flowing curly hair and visibly shapely legs, feet and genitals; women cover the hair and have no visible shape below the waist, but they expose the neck and chest.

in one endless length of fabric, so that determining the sex of any single figure on the frieze requires some scrutiny. But by the later fourteenth century, the ladies in illuminations and paintings are instantly discernible in their high, stiffened veils and long, trailing skirts, which appear in striking contrast to the articulated bodies and bushy hair of the gentlemen. In keeping with its dynamic emotional core, fashionable clothing began to display not just plain sexual difference, as traditional clothing always does, but a rich form of dramatic adversarial expression between men and women, which is one of the recurrent fictional themes of modernity in general.

In fashion, it is indeed the element of personal story, so important to modern literature and the telling of modern history, that lies behind its temporal style of formal language, behind all the effects that are forced to change so as to conform to temporal phrasing. Unlike anything else in the material world, clothing must deal with each person's body. Many may not wear one garment, as many may shelter under one roof and eat from one pot. But fashion goes still further than clothing, to engage with the idea of an individual body having an individual psyche and a particular sexuality, a unique youth and maturity, a single set of personal experiences and fantasies. This is a notion quite at odds with what the figures on the *Ara Pacis* had been suggesting, or what the whole range of garments worn in the peasant village convey. Fashion is relentlessly personal.

Although it seems to require that many people do the same thing, fashion is nevertheless committed to the idea of unique personality in the very forms it uses—the material forms generated out of unconscious fantasy, which begins in the individual psyche. It is these forms that have always seemed to make fashion ridiculous, and people ridiculous along with it: the peculiar hats, the pointed shoes, the useless appendages, the varieties of constriction, the big shoulders, the whole story; and this has consistently applied to both sexes. Art, modernizing at the same time, shows the same new personal character in the new evocative and suggestive formal vocabulary that infuses the work of the early Renaissance, the three-dimensional curves and shadows that offer compelling personal expositions in Masaccio's frescoes and Van Eyck's panels.

In emphasizing the idea of an individual body, fashion thus illustrates the idea that sexuality, with its reliance on individual fantasy and memory, governs each person's life. It illustrates collective life as if it were personal narrative, with its linear, subjective path through time. By offering extreme visions that seem to satisfy everybody for a minute, but simultaneously to offend and upset everybody, fashion itself refers obliquely to the way lust, fear, or zeal may overwhelm the moment, only to shift with the flux of days and the shift of circumstance. Fright and lust (or contempt, or self-loathing, or hatred) may make people ridiculous for the time being; but they are legitimate conditions everyone respects, especially in the modern world.

Fashion can represent emotional forces that don't have to be the direct echo of any one wearer's feelings during such a fashion's vogue. The fashion will be a collective vision; but it will use the shapes that lie in individual psychic depths, and it will be guided by available imagery in the available arts, using garments people recognize. Thus, in fashion, aggression (or boredom, or hope, or longing for childhood) will seem to be expressed by everybody's clothes for a time, even those who are not feeling those things, because it suits the prevailing temper to acknowledge them and not others in the silent theater of the mode.

By "everybody," I of course mean not really everybody, since there is now no single fashion, nor has there ever really been; but everybody in one visible group. To do this, the curves and angles of dress in several different fashions may unconsciously imitate and mock bodily forms (even lungs and intestines, or teeth and vertebrae) always in direct contact with parts of real bodies, and at the same time use recognizable garments with publicly acknowledgeable sources. The references may make a double mockery, or a doubly remote allusion.

The allusion to known imagery not only gives coherence and an acceptable public meaning to the shapes of fashion, but intervenes to edit and temper their direct effect. The picture creates the enabling distance between the wearer and the direct psychological meaning of the form; if women are actually padding their shoulders to suggest strength, or wearing masses of extremely untidy hair to suggest emotional license, they need not believe it at the time, but only see the desirability of the look as expounded in currently admired images of actresses or models, and approximated by attractive persons in the common world. Explanations of fashion are so often incomplete because the sources for the deep appeal of certain forms and styles must be hidden, in order that fashion may freely do its creative work.

Clothes that are in fashion may make the body refer to parts of itself, and to other clothed versions of itself, and to liken other objects to bodily parts. A certain sort of hat may make a person's head suggest a penis—that's fairly obvious; but other hats can make the head into a sort of fist, a possible foot, a muscle; or they may simply refer to other known hats —a railroad-worker's cap or a sunbonnet. Or, most commonly, both at once. Along with strength, padded shoulders on either sex can also bring breasts and buttocks to mind; certain pants can seem like sleeves, making legs into arms; and many have noticed that a very low-cut shoe turns a woman's instep into a chest or a back in a very low neckline, with suggestive cleavage between the first two toes.

Dressed bodies may be made to resemble bric-a-brac or plants, trash-heaps or sailboats. Strips of fabric anywhere on the body make ghost shackles or notional bandages. A sarong suggesting the South Seas may also seem like a bath towel; it may be worn with a dandified jacket evoking Beau Brummell or with a leather tunic that would go well on a medieval headsman in a thirties movie. Costume jewelry in particular is made for this sort of task, now seeming to offer nice morsels to eat or amusing handles to turn, now instruments of torture or lethal machinery, now arcane badges of office from unknown ancient cults. One style of shirt may suggest terrorism, another an earlier century or a trite fantasy about the future.

Fashion now also offers garments bearing words that play a lexical game with underlying breasts, chests, backs, bellies, and shoulders—in a semiological climate, detachable words have been added to the common stock of visual fantasy, to be mixed with body-parts and picture-parts. Fashion provides modish versions of characters from the visual arts, so that you can dress like Bart Simpson, say; but if you prefer, fashion will also let you wear a picture of Bart Simpson on your chest, or the words "Bart Simpson" instead. You can moreover dress like Van Gogh, or like one of Van Gogh's models, or you can wear a tee-shirt saying "Van Gogh" on it. You can alternatively have Van Gogh's *The Starry Night* embroidered in sequins on the back of your jacket, or his own painted face photoprinted on your leg-warmers.

Fashionable clothes thus always look personal, since the forms composing them refer to individuality, even if the clothes share in the looks of everybody else's at the moment. Fashion indeed owes its extraordinary power to the way it can make each person look truly unique, even while all the people following the mode are dressing very much alike. The deep need to be singular and the deep need to be part of a group are simultaneously fulfilled by fashion—it has always allowed you to have your cake and eat it, if you have the strength of your convictions and faith in your eye.

Even when many people wearing one fashion seem superficially to resemble one another, the suggestive configurations of modish clothing will in fact lend a further individuality to each, as general fashions can't help bringing out certain personal qualities and suppressing others. The same chic short hair will make one man look grim and another man look boyish; and a few years later, chic long hair will make the same grim one look romantic and the boyish one formidable.

Now, in the last quarter of this century, women discontented with present aspects of female fashion may simply adopt a different fashion, one of the several available that are quite unlike the feminine modes of the past. An enlightened woman may prefer to call such clothing Basic, Timeless, Purely Comfortable, and Not Fashion—but of course it still is. Unless she weaves or knits the fabric and invents every bit of the costume out of her head, fashion designers are designing any garments she buys, and the fashion business is making and marketing them, with the same energy it applies to those creations labelled with famous names that are reported in the fashion press.

But it is extremely interesting that when contemporary

women wish to be simple and timeless and outside fashion, the clothes they usually choose are traditionally masculine in origin, the pants and shirts and jackets and sweaters of modern classic male dress, jeans and flannel shirts included. Instead of aiming for any purely female basic way to dress, like some of their dress-reforming forbears in the last century, they have simply moved to partake directly of established male fashion, as women have repeatedly shown a desire to do for centuries. In this century, they have succeeded. There is apparently no present escape from women's ancient wish to wear men's clothes, turn them to female account, and to feel liberated when they do it. Why?

There is, I would claim, something perpetually more *modern* about male dress itself that has always made it inherently more desirable than female dress. It is not just the sign of power in the world, or of potency in the head, nor has it ever generally been more physically comfortable; but since the late Middle Ages, male dress also has had a certain fundamental esthetic superiority, a more advanced seriousness of visual form not suggested by the inventors of fashion for women in the past. To discover what that is, we will again have to go back a bit.

2. Early Fashion History

First, about borrowing bits of dress from the other sex. Extremely separate male and female effects in fashion, like those in 1380 or 1680, in 1850 or 1950, suggest that each sex currently wants to have a very clear sense of distance from the other one. Communities have sometimes enforced such sartorial separation with considerable rigor, making laws prohibiting transvestism and imposing stiff penalties for violations. But this usually begins to happen when the visual differences between men's and women's clothes are actually in a new state of confusion, and fashion is beginning to bring the sexes closer together after having sharply divided them. Since it is committed to sexual expression, fashion has repeatedly done this, because sexuality itself gets a sharp specific emphasis if someone uses the clothes of the other sex —especially without otherwise hiding his or her own. It is sexual *pleasure*, set up in visible defiance of the clear male and female signals designed to further procreation, that is emphasized by any hint of homoerotic fantasy in clothes; and it frightens many.

Since personal sexuality is always the engine of fashion, anything erotically disturbing will repeatedly tend to emerge on its surface, in opposition to whatever has lately been conventionally defining males and females. Sartorial borrowings from the other sex, whether individual or collective, suddenly display a modern kind of knowledge that sexuality is fluid, unaccountable and even uncomfortable, not fixed, simple and easy. Besides sex, fashion insists on risk. If the visual divide between men and women starts looking too symbolic, too untroubled, too conventional instead of dramatic, fashion will begin producing an erotic disturbance. But not, of course, always the same one.

It's therefore not surprising that mainstream feminine fashion has so often fed on the surface device of selective borrowing from men, usually in small doses, for provocative effect. But George Sand, wearing a complete man's suit in a period when sexual separateness was very intense, became an erotic icon because she looked even more feminine in her tailored jacket and trousers, not masculine — that is, she looked more sexy. Notably, she did not cut her hair or disguise her full figure: it was not drag, with the aim of illusion. By taking up men's clothes, and having them well fitted to her feminine body, she showed herself to be interested not in female concerns like child-bearing and domesticity, nor in the standard feminine uses of alluring submissiveness, but in a female erotic life that depends on an active imagination, on adventurous and multiform fantasy, the modern sort of sexuality customarily reserved for men. Because when fashion first arrived to make clothing modern, it was men's clothes that provided a field for the expression of adventurous sexual fantasy, not women's.

Modernity has obviously recurred in waves, of which only the latest is associated with the beginning of this century. Looking just at clothing since 1200, you can see that spurts of cultural advance were illustrated by the art of dress in sharp new visualizations of human looks, and that most of these were initially masculine. Women's dress reacted to new masculine sartorial assertions both with counter-assertions of exaggerated conservative and submissive elements, and more superficially with theft, especially after about 1515. Women's modes thereafter began to raid bits of male clothing as a standard ploy, an imaginative advance on extreme feminine devices. Things rarely went the other way. It's clear that the fastest and sexiest advances in Western costume history were made in male fashion, including the initial leap into fashion itself in the late twelfth century, the shift into modernity which threw down the challenge to all succeeding generations.

Until then, the European scheme for costume since late antiquity had dressed men and women in similar bag-like garments without curved seams, either for armholes or to create any fit around the body. Three-dimensionality was not built into the construction of the garment, but came into existence as the fabric fell around the wearer and was variously wrapped, belted and fastened. This sort of dress was and still is common to much of the Eastern hemisphere, in societies that do not traditionally have our sort of fashion. And in recent attempts to emulate Western dress, the people of Nepal, for example, follow the ancient rule—it is the men who strive for modernity and now wear cut and sewn Western clothes, while the women keep to the old draperies once worn by both.

During the early Middle Ages men's tunics might sometimes be shorter than women's, but both sexes wore draped clothing still fundamentally like those of the ancient Greeks and Romans, who had also allowed men shorter tunics for active war, active labor and active leisure. Men wore long gowns, too, on all formal civil occasions. The main new medieval difference between the sexes was that with their shorter tunics, men wore separate leg-coverings loosely drawn up and attached to a waistband, and loose-fitting underpants tied around under those, both arrangements well adapted to the European climate and deriving from the original Northern and Northeastern invaders of the Mediterranean world. For Greeks and Romans, they had originally had the potent chic of the forbidden, the outrageous dress of the enemy. Women's stockings, almost invisible, only came up to the knee, and women had no pants at all, even underneath. Some men's clothing thus already formed a somewhat more detailed bodily envelope than women's, even though it was all made of baggy drapes.

Art of the early Middle Ages shows how artists virtually created the beauty of early medieval clothing, inventing beautiful reciprocities of fold, fastening, texture and layer in harmony with stylized arms and legs, combining the components of the figure with abstractions of drapery just as Greek sculptors and vase-painters had done. Early medieval carvers, painters, illuminators and mosaicists were clearly more gifted for couture than the straight-cutting, straight-sewing tailors of the time. You can see modern fashion lurking in the works of art, getting ready to be born.

The first revolutionary advances in European fashion, however, were connected to the late-twelfth-century development of plate armor, which still later male fashions hastened to imitate in various ways. And although subsequent male fashion might exaggerate, compress, decorate and overburden a man's body, and wholly cover its surface, the aim of the design thereafter was nevertheless to expound the male human shape itself. The new development in armor was quite different from the style of Classical armor, which had followed the forms of the ideal nude torso and parts of the arms and legs, coating naked muscles in metal sculpture that seemed to imitate them, and leaving other parts bare.

By contrast, the dynamic formal ingenuity of medieval plate armor suggests that it was designed to enhance the articulated beauty of complete male bodies very creatively, in the modern way, with an invented abstract imagery of multifaceted brilliance and unearthly-looking strength. It was a great esthetic as well as practical advance: early medieval armor had been made of chain mail, which hung straight down like fabric, only heavily and doubtless painfully. Colored tunics were worn over it for dash and glitter as well as identification, and thick tunics underneath for protection from it; but in itself it had no way to enhance the fighting man's figure.

Innovations in armor mark the first real modernity in Western fashion, showing ways to redesign all the separate parts of the male body and put them back together into a newly created shape, one that replaced the naked human frame with another one that made a close three-dimensional, line-for-line commentary on it in another medium. Male clothing lost the unfitted character it had had since antiquity and began to suggest interesting new lines for the torso, and to consider the whole shape of legs and arms in its tailoring scheme. Plate armor moreover required an undergarment made by a linen-armorer, a close-fitting padded suit that outlined the whole man and protected him from his metal casing, of which it followed the shape. Male fashion quickly aped the shapes created by the linen-armorers, who can really count as the first tailors of Europe.

From this time on, round about 1300, clothed men and women began to look extremely different. For men, perfectly fitted tights and tight-fitting doublets were laced together around the waist for smooth overall fit, and formal coats worn over this were very short, neat and padded. Sleeves were also cut of several pieces, shaped, and padded. The separate hose were sewn together to become tights, and drawn up firmly to hide the underpants; and once legs showed all the way up, the codpiece was invented, and padded. In Italy, home of the first Classical revival, some of this articulation clearly echoed the new vogue for the antique male nude, which was also making appearances in Italian Renaissance art; but it was the startling and prestigious beauty of the armed man that most profoundly affected European fashion for centuries afterwards. Most fourteenth-, fifteenth-, sixteenth-, and early-seventeenth-century male dress tended to imitate armor in forming stiff abstract shapes around the body, finally culminating in the starched ruff at the neck, a kind of armor-like abstraction of the shirt collar.

In the same period of European history, women's clothes stayed essentially conservative, relinquishing very little, keeping to the original Classical formulas. Later women's fashion, specifically for erotic effect as we have suggested, often copied masculine *accessories*, not the whole costume. This was one feminine method for quick fashionable variety in what had been generally a slow stylistic progress up to the fifteenth century, during which the elaborate development of sleeved and fitted dresses had only gradually created feminine clothes with more shape and flair than antiquity had provided. Then, after the early sixteenth century, certain female styles of bodice, hat, collar, shoe, and sleeve were simply stolen from men, to add a new whiff of sexual daring to women's clothes without recourse either to forbidden pants or to excessive exposure. Such gestures do not aim for a real masculine effect, the look of active power; they show a desire to look erotically imaginative without looking too feminine — to mimic male sexual freedom, instead of exaggerating the look of female compliance. The whores in Urs Graf engravings of around 1514 wear their male hats with fine provocation, like Marlene Dietrich in her topper.

If Joan of Arc had appeared in male dress and male armor two hundred and fifty years earlier than she did, or one hundred and fifty years later, she might have shocked nobody by her clothes alone. But in the 1420's, her men's clothing was all the more outrageous because men's clothes were so sexually expressive. Joan was violating the strongly divided rule for fashion at the moment; the dragging skirts and tall hair-concealing headdresses of women had become much more emphatic, after men's clothes had begun to follow the lines of their bodies, to show off the complete shapes of their legs, to adopt remarkable footgear and sport their natural hair in interesting styles.

Because of the new element of divided sexual fantasy in dress, Joan looked immodestly erotic in her men's gear. She wasn't just disguised as a man, and she didn't just look soldierly and practical, especially since in her private moments without armor she was something of a dandy. At court, she seized the male privileges of going bareheaded and showing off her legs and figure with attractive tailoring, abandoning the excessively romantic modesty of current women's dress without hiding the fact that she was a woman. The result was that she seemed to be shamelessly displaying the breadth and richness of her sexual fantasies, not simply clothing her spiritual and political strength in its suitable armor. And in so doing, she clearly aroused the sexual fantasies of others. She always insisted on the necessity of her men's clothes, but she never once said they were convenient or comfortable. It all seemed to sort very ill with her spiritual ambition, and helped give her the reputation of sorceress and whore.

For centuries after the male revolution in the Middle Ages, women continued to wear variations of the dress, which was simply the same floor-length tunic of antiquity, the chiton, peplos or stola, which had then been worn with a large draped shawl used as overgarment and veil. The dress was traditionally one-piece from neck to hem, but in the Renaissance it came to be made in two sections, so that the top part, the body or bodice, could be stiffened to rhyme with the male fashions based on armor. The dress was worn with a chemise under it and (for the prosperous) a fine long robe over it for formal occasions. With this went some sort of hood, veil or kerchief on the head, symbolically if not actually covering the hair, just as in the ancient world. In cold Europe, the main difference from Mediterranean antiquity lay in the creation of close-fitting sleeves, so that the dress always covered the arms and the overgarment became a sleeved robe instead of the shawl-like drape of Greece and Rome. Sleeves, richly trimmed or not, were sometimes made separately like stockings, slipped up the arm, and laced or pinned in place.

After the dress became two-pieced in the early sixteenth century, its skirt might be a truly separate garment, most commonly called in English a petticoat. This skirt would show behind the opening of the overdress, or below it if the overdress were hitched up. Poor women might only wear a chemise, a petticoat and a sleeveless bodice, or even no bodice; but they would certainly wear a kerchief on the head. The petticoat was originally not an undergarment at all, but simply any separate skirt. As such, it became the one defining female garment, along with the veil for the head. To dress as a woman, in such a way as to be wholly transformed and disguised, all a man needed was a skirt and a kerchief. Right now these two garments will still do it — but only in Western countries.

The female costume stayed essentially the same since the Middle Ages, with eventual changes in the fitting and stiffening of the various parts of it, each of which gave temporary variation to the overall shape and harmonized with male stiffness. But the basic scheme of single undergarment (the chemise, or smock, or shift), long dress, overdress and headdress was of great antiquity and great sobriety, freighted with centuries of symbolic female modesty reaching back to the ancient world. Sleeves were always long, and originally all necklines were high. Once it began, fashion might thicken or thin out the female formula, sometimes imitating the simplicity of the poor, sometimes adding more display with extreme extensions or extra details, sometimes imitating men's accessories; but the scheme was not radically challenged until this century.

The continuity of the formula was of utmost importance, expressing the idea that fashion might keep changing, but that women remained guardians of basic assumptions, embodied principally in the universal long clothes of ancient times that men of the late Middle Ages had felt free to abandon. The refinement of the civil arts seemed to be given over to women, as long gowns became ever more exceptional and ceremonial for men. Men's new armor-like suits set the vigorous, modernizing tone for fashionable change, and set the example, giving women's dress the chance to take opposing or harmonizing shapes, to engage in the new visual dialogue of the sexes, but without abandoning anything at all.

The female image was thus perpetually founded on its own ancient past, varying its basic structure only well within the ancient rules. These had been based on ancient divine law and civil laws; and they easily took on the aura of natural law, so that when long skirts, long hair and requisite head coverings were finally given up by the women of this century, the change seemed like a profound blasphemy. Trousers, of course, were a worse one.

During the history of fashion, one can see the hidden form of the actual woman being virtually replaced by a satisfactory image of the Dressed Woman, often shaped to give her bizarre proportions according to shifts in erotic imagination as fashion kept changing, but always essentially meant to conceal her body in the ancient way, and to replace its plain facts with satisfying mythic and fictional verities. The original expressive aim of ancient female dress had been modesty, as it still is in Islam. Opposing notions of sexual attractiveness were added by fashion, in a tense counterpoint to the original principle of concealment.

Female fashion's first variation on the ancient theme of modesty was the lowering of the neckline in the fourteenth century. When he acquired more noticeable legs, she immediately acquired more noticeable breasts. This was an electrifying maneuver, accomplished without giving up the overlapping draperies that women had worn for millennia, and it was later followed by the equally electrifying stiffening of the bodice, of which one sexy effect was its imitation, as we have said, of the new effects of male armor. These female moves were certainly not independently modernizing steps; if anything they were somewhat regressive, adding an erotic narcissism to modest garments—a dimension that only emphasized their continuity. But the opening of the neckline set a precedent for feminine fashion: ever since the first medieval move toward décolletage, selective exposure of skin was to be a female theme. Although men got to be consistently more innovative with regard to overall tailoring, the whole surface of their bodies was usually covered.

Until the late seventeenth century, the modish costume for both sexes was often distracting and mobile in itself, parts of it puffed out, trailing or swinging, or elaborately embellished on the surface to draw attention away from the actual body and toward all the possibilities of fantasy; but even though male fashion might be tight and heavy, cumbersome and elaborate, the shapes of masculine dress always continued to articulate the body, to demonstrate the existence of a trunk, neck and head with hair, of movable legs, feet and arms, and sometimes genitals—whereas those of feminine dress did not. The true structure of the female body was always visually confused rather than explained by fashion. It held to the old insistence on female corporeal concealment, now offered by means of imaginative distraction and illusion.

A woman's arms and head might be fairly intelligible, but her hair was usually carefully bound up and often covered by headgear that further disguised the actual shape of her head and its normal relationship to her neck, besides editing the character of her hair itself. Her pelvis and legs were always a mystery, her feet a sometime thing, and her bosom a constantly changing theatrical presentation of some kind. Needless to say, her exposed hands were always dramatic costume elements, exciting bare episodes in a sea of fabric.

On the other hand, the design of male dress had a foundation in the structure of the whole physical body, a formal authenticity derived from human corporeal facts. Its fictions, although also given to deception and illusion, consequently had a more forceful reality than the fantasies of women's modes, especially during the long period of male license for color, invention and display.

Public attention has nevertheless always been riveted on the feminine scheme of varying the same idea in different ways through time. This has been what is meant by "Fashion" when it is despised as woman's business. The perpetual insistence on using the themes of modesty and eroticism together has provided a fascinating show, and has forever linked the idea of female fashion with falsity. But it is important to remember that despite all the differences in the ways male and female dress were formally conceived, the two sexes created a harmonious visual balance for hundreds of years, as we can see in works of art. Colors and fabrics and trimmings were similar for both sexes, and differed according to station in life and occasion, and sometimes region, but not gender; and the same was true about the degree of complexity and adornment.

One reason for this, and for everything we have so far described, was that all tailors for both sexes were men. The basic scheme for fashion was the product of a male craft, a display conceived as a two-sexed unit, a single visual illustration of the relation between men and women. Tailors moreover existed at all levels of society like cobblers and tinkers; it was not just the rich who had their clothes made. I would also hasten to emphasize that a tailor's female clients would have just as much creative say in his results as male ones would; tailors were humble artisans and not prestigious designers. The choice of colors, details and accessories was certainly a client's own business, man or woman; but the technical standard of design and construction was the same for both sexes, in the village or the city.

3. Later Changes

Given the waywardness at the core of fashion, we can see that any change in fashion must aim to create a new disequilibrium just when a vivid style has achieved a state of balance and become too easy to take. Contrary to folklore, most changes are not rebellions against unbearable modes, but against all too bearable ones. Tedium in fashion is much more unbearable than any sort of physical discomfort, which is always an ambiguous matter anyway; a certain amount of trouble and effort is a defining element of dress, as it is of all art.

In the past, stiffness, heaviness, constriction, problematic fastenings, precarious adornments and all similar difficulties in clothing would constantly remind privileged men and women that they were highly civilized beings, separated by exacting training, elaborate education and complex responsibilities from simple peons with simple pleasures, burdens and duties. Changes in very elegant fashion usually meant exchanging one physical discomfort for another; the comfort of such clothes was in the head, a matter of honor and disci-

LEFT: François Clouet, *Le Duc d'Alençon*, French, 1575. BELOW: Sánchez Coello, *Queen Anne of Austria*, Spanish, c. 1575.

His costume retains the stiffness of armor. The painting, using a plain backdrop, emphasizes his separate parts and their well-defined, wrinkle-free shapes; even the regular folds of his ruff have a metallic rigidity. Below, her collar and hat copy the male fashion, and so does her armor-like bodice; but her costume retains the traditional female formula of underdress and overdress, the sleeves of one showing under those of the other. The overdress has a front opening, here worn closed but much emphasized with braid and big knots.

pline and the proper maintenance of social degree.

One basic modern need is to escape the feeling that desire has gone stale. Fashion therefore depends on managing the maintenance of desire, which must be satisfied, but never for too long. It's easy to see how one general impulse of fashion would therefore be, for example, to make the whole body seem rigid when it had been flexible for a long time, as in the case of the armor-like garments of the Renaissance, or to reclarify the anatomical scheme, as Neo-classic fashion did when Baroque and Rococo dress had been blurring its outlines for several generations. An intermediate example appeared in the first half of the seventeenth century, which inaugurated the fashionable impulse to make existing formal schemes more casual, to create an air of accident, of unbalance, even of carelessness or perversity in the choice and wearing of familiar garments. Again, men were responsible, and women's clothes followed their example up to a point.

By 1650, armor had definitively proved itself obsolete in the field and had even lost much of its ceremonial importance; vestigial metal gorgets and breastplates might continue as badges of rank. But during the harrowing period of the Thirty Years' War and the English Civil War in the first half of the seventeenth century, the most exciting fighting man was the rough-and-ready soldier, clad in baggy breeches and a loose-fitting leather jerkin. Under this he wore a plain shirt with huge sleeves, of which bits and snatches showed through the flaps and slits in the jerkin, and the whole figure was covered in straps, buckles and buttons for attaching bits of military gear. He was accoutered with big boots, big hat, big cape and a loosely slung sword.

To echo the flavor, elegant men grew their hair long and affected swagger, loosened their collars and let their stockings wrinkle, and wrapped themselves in sweeping cloaks. An unbuttoned guard-room spirit acquired an aristocratic chic, as the English court portraits by Van Dyck or the French engravings by Jacques Callot amply show. Tight doublets and starched ruffs, clipped hair, neat footwear and padded breeches all began to look ridiculous instead of orderly and imposing. The power of perfect symmetry and containment gave way to the force of impulse and persuasion. There was, in harmony with this new Baroque mode, a general "delight in disorder," the first sartorial display of attractive nonchalance.

In the later twentieth century, we have seen a recurrence of the desire to wear open-collar or collarless shirts and abandon the necktie, to leave the hair uncut and let it flow or flop, to let stubble grow on the chin, to wear unfitted new versions of formerly tight garments, to wear unmatching versions of what used to match, and to adopt the gear of leisure moments for standard dress wear. The conscious, verbal justification of such moves is always easy; they are associated with individual freedom, honesty, and physical comfort in the face of what are suddenly seen as rigid strictures. But they are usually undertaken in fashion's abiding spirit of esthetic subversion — they are active moves toward change for its own sake, not outraged retreats from the iron demands of the mode itself. Fashion is just as severe about ease as it is about order, and loosely knotted scarves and the right degree of stubble are often much harder to manage than formal neckties and smooth shaving.

Given the long-lasting habit of conservatism in female dress, it is not surprising that the instigation of such subversive shifts, such wholesale "modernizations," should have been masculine. Although the details of women's clothing changed during these periods to echo the prevailing flavor, whether of ease or of discipline, women's dress never abandoned the décolleté dress with deceptive skirt and shaping bodice, and the elaborate headdress involving a goodly head of artfully arranged hair, its adornments often including a hood or a veil, a lace or linen cap, or a concealing bonnet, all variations on the same modest idea. Fashionable *hats* were always informal, rakish, slightly indecent for women, since all hats were either masculine or lower-class in origin.

Military costume went on to undergo many changes, and to be the source for much of the male sexuality expressed in dress ever since — to which women have continued to help themselves for interesting effects. The most recent version of the theme has not been military but athletic, with the influence of possible uses for synthetic fibers in the gear for hockey-players, skin-divers, runners, cyclists of all kinds, and racing-car drivers, but also for others who pit their bodily strength against huge odds. Male fashion takes note of mountaineers and astronauts, even extraterrestrials and travellers into the future — gamblers with the fate of the earth, as armed knights and crusaders were perceived to be in the Middle Ages. Armor-like clothing, now often made of synthetic fibers and molded plastic as well as leather, is once again sensational.

During the early-nineteenth-century wave of modernity represented by the famous Dandy mode, which we will later look at in detail, the stylistic source was also more sporting than military, founded chiefly on English country wear for hunting and shooting; and the mode itself was duly imitated in women's clothes, although not for anything other than riding clothes until this century. Until then, also, all elegant female imitations of male dress, military or not, were confined to the upper body except for shoes. The ancient skirt, which hid women from the waist down and thus permitted endless scope for the mythology of the feminine, had become a sacred female fate and privilege, especially after it became firmly established as a separate garment. Men did not wear skirts, although they might wear robes and gowns on occasion.

Trousers for respectable women were publicly unacceptable except for fancy dress and on the stage, and they were not generally worn even invisibly as underwear until well on in the nineteenth century. At that period the common adoption of underpants by women seems to represent the first expression of the collective secret desire to wear pants, only acceptably brought out on the surface with the bicycling costumes of the 1890's, and only finally confirmed in the later twentieth century with the gradual adoption of pants as normal public garments for women.

Anomalous persons like George Sand and Joan of Arc made their temporary sensations in a virtual vacuum; a few movements like that of Amelia Bloomer in the nineteenth century came and went. Pants were still a forbidden borrowing from the male, so unseemly that they could only be generally hidden until their time finally came. After those millennia of dresses, dividing the legs of respectable women with a layer of fabric seemed like sexual sacrilege. Consequently pants on women figured, naturally enough, in soft-core pornography since the eighteenth century, and they were often worn for seductive purposes by fast ladies in elegant society ever since the sixteenth. Trousers had certainly been worn by female mine-workers, fisherfolk and agricultural laborers, and naturally by dancers and acrobats, and actresses or singers in "breeches" parts; but the low status of all these female occupations kept women's pants firmly associated with lowness in general, or else with the Mysterious East, which had its own dubious associations.

The twentieth-century modernization of women was altogether a laggard development, since it came a hundred years later than the great innovations, created for men by English tailors, that still form the basis of modern male dress. At that period, just as with plate armor only better, the male body received a complete new envelope that formed a flattering modern commentary upon its fundamental shape, a simple and articulate new version that replaced the naked frame, but this time without encasing it, upholstering it, stiffening it, or overdecorating it. The modern suit, although it still hid every inch of skin, now skimmed the surface and moved in counterpoint to the body's movement, making a mobile work of art out of the combination.

At that same time female fashion was also temporarily pared down, thinned out and simplified; but it continued throughout the next hundred years with the primitive, disguising long-dress-and-careful-headdress formula. Fashion was still steadily rearranging the proportions of the female body and avoiding much reference to its actual composition, just as female costume had been doing ever since the first big trailing skirts of the fourteenth century. Nineteenth-century fashionable changes for women became even more distracting on the surface, as the changes in men's clothes continued to be a matter of subtly altering the basic tailored shape and its basic fabrics. The sartorial drama between the sexes became more acute than it had ever been.

Along with modern English woolen tailoring for men's coats, modern long trousers came into existence as another example of startling and subversive male fashion. They chiefly derived from the French Revolutionary workingman's *sans-culotte* costume, although they were also worn by

British common sailors and colonial slave-laborers, and had been occasionally used by gentlemen both for active sportswear and for leisure in those same colonies. But apart from their exciting plebeian connotations, they created an undemanding loose alternative to the close-fitting silk kneebreeches and skin-tight doeskin pantaloons of the late eighteenth century—clothes which had shown off the male legs and crotch without much room for compromise.

Trousers did not require a perfect body, and they had a nicely daring, casual look in themselves. They were instantly modified from their working-class simplicity and assimilated into the subtle tailoring scheme already developed for the elegant male coat of the new nineteenth century. The tube-like coverings for the legs answered harmoniously to the tube-like sleeves of the coat; and when the coat-skirts began consistently to veil the clearly delineated crotch of earlier days, the brilliantly colored necktie asserted itself, to add a needed phallic note to the basic ensemble.

The modern masculine image was thus virtually in place by 1820, and it has been only slightly modified since. The modern suit has provided so perfect a visualization of modern male pride that it has so far not needed replacement, and it has gradually provided the standard costume of civil leadership for the whole world. The masculine suit now suggests probity and restraint, prudence and detachment; but under these enlightened virtues also seethe its hunting, laboring, and revolutionary origins; and therefore the suit still remains sexually potent and more than a little menacing, its force by no means spent during all these many generations. Other ways for men to dress now share the scene with suits, so suits have shifted their posture; but they remain one true mirror of modern male self-esteem. Later we will follow their history and consider their fate more closely.

4. Female Invention

But meanwhile, what about women? Did their clothes contribute anything important to the successive modernizations of dress, to the true development of fashion rather than its static variation? What fundamental new things have they worn without copying men? One thing to notice first might be whether men have ever copied women, and borrowed any compelling effects from specifically female trappings.

One feminizing male theme did appear in the Renaissance, in the décolleté necklines worn for a few years around 1500 by elegant young men, like Dürer in his self-portraits of 1493 and 1498, or by the male subjects of Titian's and Giorgione's portraits during the same period. The fashion gives a strong feminine cast even to images of bearded men, since an open neckline was already a basic feature of women's clothes. It also suggests a certain vulnerability that has little to do with standard male ideals of strength and ruthlessness or of austerity and aloofness. It has a marked passive erotic flavor, and was often doubtless intended to suggest the sexual as well as the sartorial modes of antiquity.

In the late Middle Ages women's necklines could be lowered because all clothes for both sexes began to be more close-fitting; an open neck would no longer make the dress fall off. One can see why men might also use the open neck for a time as an alluring device, to give their clothes a delicate flavor suitable for gentlemen engaged in contemplative or artistic pursuits, but also to show off fine neck muscles and handsome clavicles. Even among the tough Swiss mercenaries of the early sixteenth century the low open neckline appears as a good foil to exposed hairy legs, a big padded codpiece and vigorously slashed sleeves. But this vogue was very short-lived for men, a Humanist fashion connected with the revival of ancient learning and ancient bodily preoccupations, but unsuitable in succeeding generations devoted to religious strife and the spread of modern empire.

Although it has sometimes looked feminine to unaccustomed eyes, the long loose hair often worn by men was recurrently adopted (sometimes in wig form) as a feature of basic masculinity, Samson-style, not as a feminine touch. Loose, free hair was in fact rarely used by women without any elaboration or other head-dressing elements. The long hair of women was braided, knotted up, curled up, and interwoven with trimmings or covered: during the history of the West, only the Virgin and other virgins normally wore completely undressed long hair when fashionably dressed up.

Loose female hair was always a specifically sexual reference, the sign of female emotional looseness and sensual susceptibility, and a standard sexual invitation — Mary Magdalene wears it. This is still the case in current fashion, another sign of female reliance on ancient themes. Like female sexual desire, loose hair in the past was a potent female attribute not correctly displayed in public. But respectable unmarried girls, just like the Virgin Mary, wore loose hair to suggest the power of absolute female chastity. Their desire was unawakened like that of children, and their cloak of hair was a pure gift from God like the clothing of the field-lilies, a kind of Edenic, surrogate nudity. Unawakened desire in a full-grown girl is moreover undissipated and unadulterated, full-strength and ready, a powerful asset. Queen Elizabeth I wore loose hair at her coronation, along with pounds of jewels and brocade, to advertise her virgin status as part of her power, both sexual and temporal. Brides also wore it. Virgin saints in pictures wear it. Respectable matrons might even have their portraits painted with their hair down, in a double feminine ploy suggesting both domestic chastity and erotic potency at the same time. For most women, it was necessary to *have* long thick hair, so as to be seen to have sexuality, but to show it publicly under very strict control.

By contrast, loose hair for mature men was usually a public virile ornament, akin to the display of muscle and stature, a sign of sexual force in action. It only looks feminine when it first becomes modish, after an extended short-haired period in male fashion. Then long hair gets the immediate disapproval of conservative observers who still associate it with female license. As is so often the case, what was an ancient sign of public strength in men was a sign of personal vulnerability in women; and some of that rubs off on men when they first adopt long hair—or indeed when fashion shifts the other way, and they begin to stop liking it. Some of the free-swinging loose hair of modern women can even count as another male borrowing in these enlightened times, just like their very, very short haircuts. It can now be one way to show pure sexual strength without admitting any mythological feminine weaknesses.

Clever décolletage, on the other hand, can be counted as a truly serious and thoroughly female contribution to fashion. It includes not only the neckline, front and back, but the line at which sleeves are cut to expose the wrist or any part of the arm and shoulder. Eventually the final modernization in this vein was the irreversible shortening of the skirt itself in this century, an act performed in several stages, just like the earlier ones exposing the upper body. In that vein, the latest modern female move has been the baring of the midriff—a new option, not a necessity.

Curiously enough, the most extreme shortening of skirts has seemed to bring women's clothing full circle once again, back into the sphere of men. The very, very short skirt appeared in the 1960's just at the time that pants became generally universal for women; and the miniskirt appeared belatedly to echo the scandalous exposure of male legs in the late Middle Ages—another male borrowing from the beginning of modernity in fashion. Girls acquired a page-boy look, with endless legs in bright tights descending below tiny little tunics.

Interesting exposure above the waist, however, was the most important female initiative in fashion for centuries; and male fashion has rarely imitated it, for neck or arms or midriff. Modern men's short-sleeved formal shirts, often forbidden in strictly correct circumstances, have their disturbing flavor partly because they were really borrowed from women, for whom arm exposure is respectable. Men have allowed themselves to take their shirts off, or to roll up the sleeves and unbutton the collar, in negligent or hearty moods; but they have not been moved to cut open the neckline or cut the sleeves so as to expose the skin in interesting ways. Nor did they ever do so with coats, gowns and doublets, all during fashion's long history. Even very short shorts for men, along with skin-exposing undershirts, both quite recently adopted, are also slightly disturbing as public male garments for city wear — I believe because they also have dared to borrow the modern female rule for ordinary exposure. In antiquity, of course, it went the other way: men were bare and women covered.

Skirts, those great traditional garments, also count as an original and purely female element, when they hang from the waist. Since their beginnings in the sixteenth century, they have never been borrowed for normal male dress. The kilt, the male garment that looks most like a skirt, is in fact

LEFT: Anthony Van Dyck, *Henri II de Lorraine, duc de Guise*, 1634. BELOW: Anthony Van Dyck, *Henrietta Maria of France, Queen of England, with her Dwarf*, mid-1630's.

The duke's flowing hair, big feathery hat, big drooping collar and crumpled cloak and boots further relax a loose-fitting costume that no longer crisply models the body's separate parts. The painted terrain behind him adds still more wildness and asymmetry to the fashionably casual effect. Below, the queen now fingers the mobile folds of her skirt, instead of grasping a handkerchief. Her very low neckline has been topped off with a dashing masculine collar, and her hat and coiffure also echo the male mode; but her naked forearms are a new and purely feminine accessory. The painter has given them great prominence, along with the tactile pleasure her hands are feeling from the satin and the monkey's fur.

4. Female Invention 47

Jan Vermeer, *Man and Woman Drinking Wine*, Dutch, c. 1660.

This Dutch bourgeoise wears a conservative version of advanced feminine fashion, still not essentially altered since the Renaissance, with no male references and a modest stiffened veil covering her hair. The new, dropped shoulder-line of her dress ensures that her arms are held close to her body, even while it exposes more skin above; she has no mobile accessories. Her male companion, by contrast, may fling his great cape around him, stick out his elbows and flaunt his great white collar and cuffs, his great black hat.

a survival from the ancient days of general masculine drapery even for war. All the interesting female headgear developed from the veil into coifs and stiffened hoods of remarkable kinds was another female invention, and it was never imitated by men at all. If scholars and old men sometimes wore female-looking fitted caps to keep out the cold, they wore honorable male hats on top of them when they went out. Male hoods and cowls were either clerical, like gowns, or an unfashionable plebeian protection against weather. Now we see them on sweatshirts and parkas.

General progress in purely female modernization was slow. Although the neckline began exposing the chest quite early, the shortening of the sleeve was not accomplished until the seventeenth century, when the forearm was cautiously bared for the first time. Arms were eventually exposed to the elbow, echoed by further exposure up above, as the neckline was hugely widened and bare shoulders rose up out of it. In fashion at that moment around 1660, the naked feminine wrist and soft forearm, so suggestive of more smooth softness inside the clothes, had finally made a clear link with the naked chest and shoulders; it was another electrifying and irreversible move.

The impulse continued toward extreme exposure for the whole upper body, accompanied by even more extreme upholstery and drapery for the lower half. The idea culminated in the fashionable evening dresses of the later nineteenth century, when the whole arm was exposed along with most of the chest, back and shoulders, and the sleeves of the evening dress became vestigial. The rib-cage and waistline were strictly compressed while the elaborate skirt took on ever more shape, scope and density.

The woman was thus even more emphatically divided into top and bottom. The fashion went to final extremes in the mid-twentieth-century revival, when the sleeve was wholly discarded and the strapless dress invented, with a tight chrysalis encasing the ribs and bust above a sweeping or clinging skirt, the arms now fully exposed to include not only naked back, chest and shoulders, but also naked armpits. The theme of nearly nude top and very shrouded bottom remains compelling in the present world, and it seems suitable for moments when the historical and romantic view of women has license to prevail — at the ball or the wedding, and often on the stage or screen.

It corresponds to one very tenacious myth about women, the same one that gave rise to the image of the mermaid, the perniciously divided female monster, a creature inherited by the gods only down to the girdle. Her voice and face, her bosom and hair, her neck and arms are all entrancing, offering only what is benign among the pleasures afforded by women, all that suggests the unreserved, tender and physically delicious love of mothers even while it seems to promise the rough strife of adult sex. The upper half of a woman offers both keen pleasure and a sort of illusion of sweet safety; but it is a trap. Below, under the foam, the swirling waves of lovely skirt, her hidden body repels, its shapeliness armed in scaly refusal, its oceanic interior stinking of uncleanness.

It is really no wonder that women seeking a definitive costume in which to enact their definitive escape from such mythology should choose trousers. Articulating female legs at last must have seemed — no doubt unconsciously, since the original arguments were all about convenience — a necessary move in the theater of sexual politics. Demonstrating women's full humanity was essential; and that meant showing that they had bodies not unlike men's in many particulars. To show that women have ordinary working legs, just like men (not exquisite machines for dancing and acrobatics, flashing under tinselly froth, nor seductive members like nether arms that entice only to clasp and strangle), was also to show that they have ordinary working muscles and tendons, as well as spleens and livers, lungs and stomachs, and, by extension, brains.

Notes

1. Form and Sexuality
page line
- **1** 1 **acting as the illustrator of** 「〜を明示するものとしての役割を演じている」
  - 3 **tame collective fantasy into a fixed shape** [which is] **meant to last** last 「持続する」
  - 4 **prodding** 「刺激する」
    keep on 「〜し続ける」
  - 5 **old** 「全く」 賞賛や是認を表す形容詞の後に付く強意語。
  - 6 **need** 「心理的欲求」
    moves away from 〜 toward... 「〜から...へと移る」
  - 7 **incantation** 「呪文」
    saga 「北欧伝説」
    compact 「簡潔な」
  - 8 **phrasing** 「言いまわし」
  - 11 **the prevailing esthetic spirit** 「その場合の支配的な美的精神」
  - 12 **conflict** 「(弁証法的) 対立」
  - 13 **the look of dissatisfied search** 「探し求めても満足した結果が得られなかったという様子」
  - 15 **if and when** = if.
  - 16 **the posture of imaginative vigilance** 「想像力を働かそうとする態度」
  - 19 **abstract suits** 「抽象的なスーツ」
    When rightly managed = When balanced and coherent simplicity is rightly managed.
- **2** 1 **vibrant** 「ぞくぞくするような」
    dull 「退屈な」
  - 2 **charged with** 「〜で充満している」
  - 4 **at play** = in play. 「よく見られる」

2 5 **sexuality** 「性衝動」
　　5-**expressive motor** 「表現力」
　　6 **underlying** 「根源的な」
　　7 **waywardness** 「つむじ曲がり」
　　8 **regressive** 「退行的な」
　 10 **function** 「職務」
　　sexual mode 「性の形態」
　 12 **noble** 「貴族の」
　 13 **expounded** 「詳細に提示した」
　 15 [**were**] **tempered to** 「～するように調整された」
　　dimensions of life 「生活次元」
　 17 *seductiveness* 「性的誘惑」
　　This last 前の "*seductiveness*" を指す。
　 21 **that is** = namely. 「すなわち」
　 24-**got fully under way** 「完全に進歩をとげた」
　 27 **on which ornament provided the interest** 「装飾品が興趣を添えた」
　　began *l*.25 の "Elegant clothes" が主語。

3 1 **constriction** 「しめつけ」
　　torso 「胴体」
　　2 **trailing length** 「ひきずるほどの長さ」
　　5 **cut and fit** 「裁断の仕方と着具合」
　　7 **extra fabric** 「余分の布地」
　　8 **kinetic** 「動的な」
　　9 **went against the force of practical need** 「実際の必要性に反した」
　 10 **well beyond** 「かなり～以上に」
　　for simple ostentation 「単に見せびらかすためだけの」
　 11 **be smoothly packed away** 「凹凸がなく包み隠された」
　 12 [**might be**] **referred to on the surface** 「表面でそれと察せられる」
　 16 **festoons** 「花綱」
　 17 **with a reference suggesting that** 「～ということをほのめかしながら」
　 21 **pictorial** 次の "fashion" の補語。
　 23-**promulgated** 「広められた」

3 25 **miniatures** 「細密画」

25–**make** {
- **a bodice** (O) **so smooth,** (C)
- **the chest above** (O) **so uniformly waxen,** (C)
- **shoulders** (O) **so boneless** (C)
- **pearls** (O) **so perfectly draped** (C)
}

 27 **perfectly draped** 「申し分なく飾られた」
  Life 「人生」

4 2 **referring to** 「～に頼る」
 3–**in the new representational force of fashion** 「ファッションの新しい表現力に」 これは前の "lay deeper than that" の説明。
 6 **figure [which] dress could make them a part of**
 7–**It...that** 強調構文。
 9 **allusively** 「隠喩的に」
 10 **suggestive applied forms** 「示唆に富み，実利的機能を主とした形」
 10–**in a dynamic counterpoint to** 「～と著しく対照をなして」
 12 **done [this].**
 12–**making its own agreement with** 「～と自ら折り合いをつけて」
 13–**to create a vital sequence in its own medium** 「それ自身のメディアに活力に満ちた連続物を作るために」
 16 **In harmony with** 「～と調子を合わせて」
 17 **three-dimensional** 「立体感を与える」
 18 **program** 「番組」 *l*.20 の "a drama" を参照。
 19–**with the added status of reported facts** 「伝聞による事実という状態が付け加わった」
 21–**figures and characters** 「絵画の人物や舞台の登場人物」
 24 **overlapping and simultaneous themes** 前行の "demonstrate" の目的語。
 24–**temporality and contingency** 「一時性と偶然性」
 25 **social placement** 「社会的立場」
 26 **always cast in the terms of sexuality** 「セクシュアリティの点から常に作られた」 前行の "themes" を修飾する。

4 27 **hers or his** 「女性あるいは男性の身体」 前の"the living body"「生身の体」の説明。
5 1 **suggestive** 下行の"bodily shapes"を「連想させる」
  2 **on** 前行の"on"と並列の関係。*l*.3の"on"も同じ構文。
  2-**variable piquancy** 「変わりやすい魅力」
  5 **phrasing through time** 「時を通して台詞を言う」
  7 **framed by** 「～によって額縁をはめられた」"picture"を修飾。
  9 **an earlier way** [to look]
  10 **sleek** 「優雅な」
  12 **sash** 「スカーフ」
  13 **dramatic sequence** 「劇的連続」
  14-**Rich and poor effects** 「素晴らしい効果とみすぼらしい効果」
  15-**the representational medium of fashion** 「ファッションという表現メディア」
  16-**construction** 「解釈」 動詞は construe。
  17-**Crudity** 「未熟」
  18 **refinement** [might be]
   tacky 「安っぽい」
  21 **an acknowledged aim** 「公認の目的」
  24 **does** = comes.
  25 **confident** 「確かな」
  26 **brilliant moments of clarified vision** 「視野が明らかになった輝かしい時間」
6 1 **by vigilance** 前の"sustained"に続く。
  3 *ad hoc* 「場あたり的に」
  3-**make a medium for** 「～のメディアとなる」
  4 **it** = beauty.
  4-**make the beauty of an image seem identical with the beauty of a garment** 「あるイメージの美を衣服の美と同じだと思わせる」
  9 **having worked up to it** 「それまで進んできた」
  11 **sexual divide** 「男女の区分」
  12 **created** 主語は"the borrowing...divide"。
   suggestive 「わいせつな」,「きわどい」
  13 **done** = created.

6 14-**Small suggestions of transvestism** 「服装倒錯を少しでもほのめかすこと」 Cf. 注 *p*.16, *l*.7.
　16 **worked** = took place. 「起こった」
　18 **relief sculptures** 「浮き彫り彫刻」
　19 **drapery** 「ドレーパリー」
　　 compositions 「美術作品」
　22 **scheme for clothes** 「衣装体系」
　23 *Ara Pacis* 「平和の祭壇」
　23-**the Emperor Augustus** 「アウグストゥス皇帝」 （63B.C.–A.D.14) ローマ帝国の初代皇帝。
　25 **frieze** 「（家具などの） 帯状装飾」
　　 awash in 「～で充満している」

9　2 **requires some scrutiny** 「ある程度つくづくとながめる必要がある」
　3 **illuminations** 「（写本などの）彩飾」
　5-**in striking contrast to** 「～と著しく対照的に」
　6 **the articulated bodies and bushy hair** 「手と脚がどれかが明確にわかる身体とふさふさした髪」
　10 **adversarial** 「敵対関係の」
　11-**modernity in general** 「モダニティ一般」
　13-**it is...that** 強調構文。Cf. *p*.4, *ll*.7–8.
　14 **the telling** 「語り」
　17 **temporal phrasing** 「束の間の言葉遣い」
　17-**the material world** 「物質界」
　21 **to engage with** 「～と関わりを持つ」 前の "goes still further" の具体例。
　24 **at odds with** 「～と食い違って」
　27 **convey** この主語は "the whole range of garments worn in the peasant village"。
　　 relentlessly 「断固として」

10　1 **it** = fashion.
　2 **committed to** 「～と深く関わって」,「～に打ち込んで」
　3-**the material forms** [which are] **generated out of ...** これは前の "the very forms" の説明。

10　6　[make] people ridiculous
　　7　**along with it**　「そのほかに」
　　　　peculiar　「一風変わった」
　　　　the pointed shoes　「先のとがった靴」
　　8　**the varieties of constriction**　「身体を締め付けるさまざまなもの」
　　　　the big shoulders　「大きな肩パット」
　　9　**the whole story**　「一部始終」
　　11　**evocative and suggestive**　「喚起的で暗示的な」
　　12　**formal vocabulary**　「形についての語彙」
　　　　infuses　「〜を満たす」
　　14　**compelling personal expositions**　「いやおうなしに個をあらわにするもの」
　　　　Masaccio [məzá:tʃiou]　「マザッチョ」（1401-28?）イタリアの画家。初期ルネサンス絵画様式の確立者。
　　　　frescoes　「フレスコ画」
　　15　**Van Eyck** [vən aik]　「ファン・アイク」　Hubert（1370-1426), Jan（1385?-1441）の二人の兄弟。ともにフランドルの画家で北方ルネサンス絵画の完成者。
　　　　panels　「パネル画」　板に描いた絵。
　　16　**the idea of an individual body**　「個としての身体という考え方」
　　17　**with its reliance on individual fantasy and memory**　「個人の空想や記憶に依存するゆえに」
　　19　**collective life**　「集団構成員に共通の人生」
　　　　personal narrative　「個人的な物語」
　　23　**refers obliquely to the way**　「〜する仕方を間接的に言っている」
　　24　**the flux of days**　「日々の変化」
11　7　**garments** [which] **people recognize**
　　11　**in the silent theater of the mode**　「服装の流行という無声劇場」
　　14　**nor has there** [any fashion] **ever really been;**
　　15　**but** [I mean] **everybody in one visible group.**
　　17　**mock** = mimic.　「からかって真似する」
　　18　**vertebrae**　「脊椎」
　　23　**gives coherence and an acceptable public meaning to the shapes of fashion**　give A to B の構文。

11 25 **but** *l*.23 の "not only" と連結している。
　　edit and temper　「手を加え，和らげる」
　26 **the enabling distance**　「利用を可能にする距離」
　27 **the direct psychological meaning of the form**　「その形が有している直接的な心理的意味」
12 　2–**license**　「放らつ」，「放縦」
　　3–**the desirability of the look**　「望ましい外観」
　　4 **expounded**　「説明されている」
　　5 **approximated**　「似せられている」
　　6 **in the common world**　「普通の世界で」
　10 **refer to**　「～をほのめかす」
　11–**to liken**　「なぞらえる」 これは "may" に続くので，to は本来なら不要。
　14–**a possible foot**　「足と考えてもよさそうなもの」
　16 **sunbonnet**　「婦人用日除け帽」
　17 **Along with**　Cf. *p*.10, *l*.7.
　18 **bring...to mind**　「～を思い出させる」
　20 **low-cut**　「履き込みの浅い」
　21 **instep**　「足の甲」
　　a chest or a back　「胸か背中」
　　in a very low neckline　「ドレスの襟ぐりが非常に大きくあいた」
　22 **suggestive cleavage between the first two toes**　「足の親指と人差し指が胸の谷間のように見えること」を言っている。
　23 **bric-a-brac**　「骨董品」
　24 **trash-heaps**　「屑の山」
　25 **make**　「～になる」
　　notional bandages　「架空の巻き布」
　　sarong　「サロン」 マレーシアやジャワの人々が着用する腰布。
　27 **dandified**　「めかしこんだ」
　27–**Beau Brummell**　「だて男ブランメル」 George Bryan Brummell（1778–1840）。ジョージ4世のお気に入りで，流行の範を示しただて男。
13 　1 **tunic**　「チュニック」，「上着」
　　2 **headsman**　「首切り役」

13　2　**a thirties movie**　「1930 年代の映画」
　　　Costume jewelry　「衣服用模造宝石」
　　　in particular　「特に」
　　5　**arcane badges of office**　「神秘的な儀式のバッジ」
　　6　**cults**　「教団」
　　7　**another** [style of shirt may suggest] **an earlier century**
　　　trite　「ありふれた」
　　10　**a lexical game**　「言葉遊び」
　　　underlying　「服の下にある」
　　11　**in a semiological climate**　「記号学的風潮の中で」
　　　detachable words　「文脈から切り離せる言葉」
　　12　**the common stock**　「ありふれたストック」
　　14　**modish versions**　「モード版」
　　15　**Bart Simpson**　アメリカの漫画に登場するぎょろ目のキャラクター。
　　　say = for example.
　　18　**Van Gogh**　「ヴァン・ゴッホ」(1853-90)　オランダの画家。
　　20　*The Starry Night*　『星月夜』(1889)　ゴッホの作品。
　　21　**sequins**　「シークイン」　婦人服の装飾などに用いるスパンコール。
　　25　**share in the looks of everybody else's**　「他のどの人とも同じ外見である」
　　26　**owes... to ~**　「…を~に負うている」
14　2　**deep**　「痛切な」
　　　singular　「類のない」,「特異な」
　　4　**to have your cake and eat it**　"You cannot eat your cake and have it."「両方うまいことはできない」という意味の成句からでている。
　　7-**the suggestive configurations of modish clothing**　「最新モードの衣服をいろいろなイメージを連想させるように組み合わせて着こなすこと」
　　9　**bringing out**　「引き出す」
　　10　**others** = other personal qualities.
　　13　**formidable** = causing fear or dread.
　　15　**present aspects**　「現代の状況」
　　17　**the feminine modes**　「女性モード」
　　20　**is** [fashion]

14 20 **she** *l*.17 の "an enlightened woman"。
  23 **applies** 「注ぐ」
  25 **fashion press** 「ファッション誌」
15 4 **flannel** 「フラネル」,「ネル」 紡毛糸を主とする毛織物。
  6 **forbears** = forebears. 「先輩」
  7 **partake directly of** 「〜を直接受け継ぐ」
  11 **turn them to female account** 「男性の服を女性が利用する」
  14 **inherently** 「本質的に」
  19 **seriousness** 「深い思想性」

2. Early Fashion History

16 1 **bits of dress** = pieces of dress.
  2 **effects** 「体裁」,「外見」
  4 **currently** 「一般に」
  6 **sartorial** 「衣装の」
  7 **transvestism** 「服装倒錯」 男性あるいは女性が異性の服を着ること。
  8 **visual** 「視覚上の」,「目で見た」
  12 **is committed to** 「〜とかかわりあっている」
  13 **gets a sharp specific emphasis** 「特別鋭く目立つ」
  15 **especially without otherwise hiding his or her own** 「異性の服を着たこと以外には自分の性を隠さない場合に特にそうである」
  16 **set up** 「立てられた」
  17 **further** 「〜を促進する」,「〜を助長する」
  18 **homoerotic** = homosexual.
17 1 **engine** 「中心的原動力」
  2 **anything erotically disturbing** 「性愛的に常軌を逸脱したもの」
  4 **Sartorial borrowings** 「衣装の拝借」
  5 **whether individual or collective** 前の "Sartorial borrowings" を修飾する。
  6 **knowledge** 「理解」,「認識」
  8 **insists on** 「せがむ」,「強要する」
  8 **risk** 「冒険」

17　11　an erotic disturbance　「常軌からの性的逸脱」
　　14　has...fed on　「～にはぐくまれた」
　　15　in small doses　「少しずつ」
　　15-for provocative effect　「扇情的な効果をねらって」
　　16　George Sand　「ジョルジュ・サンド」(1804-76)フランスの女性作家で, 男装をしたことで知られる。
　　18-tailored　「男仕立ての」
　　21　drag　「男装」
　　25　feminine uses　「女性特有の効果」
　　26-adventurous　「大胆な」
　　27　multiform　「多様な」
18　　5-only the latest　「ごく最近のもの」
　　　7　spurts　「ほとばしり」
　　10　initially　「まず手始めに」
　　11　counter-assertions　「反論」
　　13　theft　「(男性服から意匠を)盗むこと」
　　14-as a standard ploy　「常套手段として」
　　20　threw down the challenge to　「～に挑戦状をたたきつけた」
　　22　the European scheme for costume　「ヨーロッパの衣装体系」
　　24　armholes　「袖ぐり」
　　25　fit　「(衣服の)合い具合」
　　26　construction　前の文との関連で, このように建築用語が用いられているが, ここでは「制作」の意味。
19　　5　emulate　「まねる」
　　　9　both　= both sexes.
　　17-loosely drawn up　「ゆるく引き寄せられた」
　　18　loose-fitting　「ゆったりした」
　　22　they　= both arrangements.
　　23　potent chic　「強い魅力」
　　27　more detailed bodily envelope　「もっと身体の各部位に応じて体を包むもの」
20　　1　baggy　「袋のようにだぶだぶした」
　　　4　reciprocities　「相互関係」衣服を画布に写実的に再現すること。
　　　　 fold, fastening, texture and layer　「ひだ, 結び目, 生地, 衣服の層」

20　5　**stylized**　「様式化された」
　　5-**the components of the figure**　「身体の構成要素」
　　6　**abstractions of drapery**　「ドレーパリーの抽象的な構図」
　　8　**illuminators**　「(写本などの) 彩飾師」
　　9　**couture** [kutúər]　「婦人服デザイン」
　　　　straight-cutting, straight-sewing　「直線裁ち, 直線縫い」
　　14　**plate armor**　「板金鎧」
　　16　**compress**　「服の中に押し込める」
　　16-**overburden**　「服を着させすぎる」
　　18　**expound**　「写し取る」
　　21　**torso**　「トルソ」　頭, 手足のない, 胴体だけの彫像。
　　22　**coating...in ～**　「～で...をおおう」
　　25-**the articulated beauty**　「明確な美」
　　27-**multifaceted**　「多面体の」

21　1　**unearthly-looking**　「この世のものと思われなく見える」
　　3　**chain mail**　「鎖かたびら」
　　5　**for dash and glitter**　「見栄ときらびやかさのために」
　　6　**identification**　「身分の確認」
　　7　**from it** = from the chain mail.
　　14　**line-for-line**　「一行ごとの」, 「詳細な」
　　15　**the unfitted character** [which] **it** [= male clothing] **had had**
　　16　**began**　前行の "lost" と並列。
　　17　**to consider**　began to $\begin{cases} \text{suggest} \\ \text{consider} \end{cases}$
　　17-**tailoring scheme**　「服を仕立てる計画」
　　18　**Plate armor**　既出。Cf. *p*.20, *l*.14.
　　19　**linen-armorer**　「リンネル武具師」
　　　　close-fitting　「体にぴったり合う」
　　20-**metal casing**　「金属の覆い」
　　21　**of which it followed the shape** = and the undergarment followed the shape of the metal casing.
　　22　**aped** = imitated.
　　23　**count**　「～とみなされる」
　　26　**fitted tights**　「体の線にあうように仕立てられたタイツ」

21 26 **tight-fitting**　「体にぴったり合う」
　　　　doublets　「ダブレット」　腰のくびれた胴衣。15～17世紀頃の男性の軽装。
　　27 **for smooth overall fit**　「円滑な動きが可能な，つなぎ服にするために」
22 　1 **neat**　「さっぱりした」
　　 2 **shaped**　「身体に合わせられる」
　　 3 **hose** [houz]　「長靴下」
　　 5 **all the way up**　「ずっと上まで」
　　　　codpiece　「股袋」　男子のズボンの前空きを隠すための袋。
　　 7 **articulation**　「身体の部分の明確な表現」
　　 8–**Italian Renaissance**　14～17世紀における古典文化の復興運動。
　　 9–**it...that**の構文。Cf. *p.*9, *l.*13.
　　14 **ruff**　「ひだ襟」
　　15 **abstraction**　「抽象化」
　　17 **relinquishing very little**　「手放すものはほとんどなく」
　　23 **elaborate**　「精妙な」
　　25 **shape and flair**　「格好とセンスのよさ」
　　27 **bodice**　「婦人服の胴着」
23 　1 **whiff**　「気味」
　　　　daring　「大胆さ」
　　 2–**without recourse either to...or to...**　「AかBに頼らずに」
　　 3 **gestures**　「衣服の修整」
　　 4 **the look of active power**　"a real masculine effect" と同格。
　　 6 **to mimic**　前行の "a desire" に続く。
　　 7 **female compliance**　「素直な女性らしさ」
　　 7–**Urs Graf**　「ウルス・グラフ」(1485-1527) スイスの彫刻家。
　　 8–**with fine provocation**　「見事に挑発しながら」
　　 9 **Marlene Dietrich**　「マルレーネ・ディートリッヒ」(1901-92) ドイツ生まれの映画女優・歌手。
　　　　topper　「シルクハット」
　　10 **Joan of Arc**　「ジャンヌダルク」(1412-31)
　　14 **all the more outrageous**　「なおさらふらちであった」
　　14–**were so sexually expressive**　「非常に性的であった」

23 16 **at the moment**　「当時の」
　　18 **emphatic**　「著しく目立つ」
　　19 **show off**　「見せびらかす」
　　20 **remarkable footgear**　「驚くべき履き物」
　　20-**sport their natural hair in interesting styles**　「生まれつきの髪をおもしろい髪型にしてみせびらかす」
　　22-**the new element of divided sexual fantasy in dress**　「性的ファンタジーが男女の別によって衣服に割り振られる，というこの新しい要素」
　　23 **gear** = clothes.
　　25 **practical**　「活動的な」
　　26 **something of**　「ちょっとした〜」
24 4-**the breadth and richness of**　「豊かな〜」
　　10 **sort very ill with**　「〜と，とても調和しない」
　　11 **helped [to] give**
　　15 **chiton** [káitn]　「キトーン」　一種の長上着。
　　　peplos　「ペプロス」　古代ギリシャの婦人の外衣。キトーンの上に重ねる。
　　　stola　「ストラ」　古代ローマの婦人が用いた外衣。キトーンと同じ型で，チュニックの上に着る。
　　16 **draped shawl**　「ドレーパリーのショール」
　　　overgarment　「上着」
　　17 **hem**　「裾」
　　18 **in two sections**　「ツーピースに」
　　19-**rhyme with**　「〜と一致する」，「〜と呼応する」
　　21 **the prosperous**　「富裕な女性たち」
　　22-**With this went some sort of hood**　倒置になっている。go with「〜に伴う」
　　23 **kerchief**　「スカーフ」
　　23-**if not actually**　「実際にではなくとも」　挿入句。
　　26 **lay in**　「〜にあった」
　　　close-fitting　「ぴっちりした」
25 2 **robe**　「ローブ」　裾まで垂れる長いゆるやかな外衣。
　　 3 **richly trimmed or not**　「豪華に飾り付けられているものも，そう

でないものも」
25　4 [were] slipped up the arm 「腕の上に滑らせて」
　　laced 「紐で結ばれて」
　5 in place 「適当な位置に」
　6 became two-pieced 「ツーピースになった」
　9 show behind...or below 「〜の後や下で見える」
　　the opening 「開口部」
　10 were hitched up 「持ち上げられた」
　14 any 「どの〜でも」
　　As such 「そういうものだから」
　14-the one defining female garment 「女性を定義する唯一の衣服」
　15 along with 「〜と一緒に」
　18 do it 「効を奏する」
　21 eventual 「偶発的な」
　　fitting 「寸法合わせ」
　21-stiffening 「(衣服の芯などを) 固くすること」
　23 harmonized　前行の"gave"と並列。
　25 smock 「スモック」 婦人用肌着。次の"shift"も同様なもの。
　　overdress 「オーバードレス」 ドレスの上に着る薄物のドレス。
　25-headdress 「ヘッドドレス」,「頭飾り」
　26 of great antiquity and great sobriety 「はるか古代からのもので,大変謹厳なもの」
　26-freighted with 「〜を背負った」
　27 reaching back to 「〜までさかのぼる」
26　2 high 「(ネックラインが) 浅い」
　2-thicken or thin out the female formula 「女性らしさの様式を濃厚にするか薄める」
　　4 display 「装飾」
　4-with extreme extensions or extra details 「極端にある部分を延ばしたり,細部を余計に付け足したりして」
　　6 scheme 「衣装体系」
　　was not radically challenged 「過激な申し立てをされなかった」
　10 basic assumptions 「基本理念」
　10-embodied principally in 「〜に主として具現されている」

26　12　**that men...**　long clothes にかかる関係代名詞節。
　　13　**the civil arts**　「市民芸術」　ただしここでの"arts"は「衣服」のこと。
　　13-**given over to**　「〜に譲渡される」
　　15-**set the vigorous, modernizing tone for fashionable change**　「ファッションの変化を起こすための近代化の方向を力強く決定づけた」
　　16-**set the example**　「手本となる」
　　21　**only well within**　「まさしく〜の中だけで」
　　22　**divine law**　「神の掟」
　　23　**civil laws**　「市民法」
　　　　took on　「獲得した」,「おびた」
　　　　aura　「独特な雰囲気」
　　23-**natural law**　「自然法」
　　24　**requisite**　「必須の」
　　26　**blasphemy**　「罰当たりの行為」
27　 8　**expressive aim**　「表現目的」
　　10　**in a tense counterpoint to**　「〜と全く好対照をなして」
　　10-**the original principle of concealment**　「隠蔽という本来の原則」
　　12　**variation**　「変化」
　　14　**he**　「男性」
　　　　she　「女性」
　　15-**an electrifying maneuver**　「大した妙策」
　　16-**the overlapping draperies**　「ドレーパリーの重ね着」
　　17　**for millennia**　「何千年ものあいだ」,「大昔から」
　　21-**if anything**　「それどころかむしろ」
　　24　**their** = of modest garments.
　　　　the opening　「広く開いたこと」
　　24-**set a precedent for**　「〜の前例を作った」
　　26　**décolletage**　「デコルタージュ」　首と肩の露出。
　　　　selective exposure of skin　「肌を選択的に露出すること」
28　 3　**the modish costume**　「流行の服装」
　　 4　**distracting**　「焦点が定まらず」
　　　　mobile　「変わりやすい」
　　 9　**elaborate**　「複雑な」

28 10 articulate 「はっきりさせる」
trunk 「胴体」
14 held to 「～に執着した」,「～を守った」
15 female corporeal concealment 「女性の身体の隠蔽」
15-by means of imaginative distraction and illusion 「想像力によって現実の姿から目をそらさせ,幻想を与えることによって」
17 intelligible 「明瞭だ」
20 besides 「～のうえに」
20-editing the character of 「～の性質を変える」
21 pelvis 「骨盤」
22 a sometime thing 「時々見られるもの」
23 theatrical presentation 「芝居の上演」
25 exciting bare episodes 「衣装をまとわない,刺激的な場面の一コマ」
29 1 fictions 「作り事」,「虚構性」
2 given to 「～したがる」,「～にふける」
4 of male license for 「男性が～を自由に利用していた」
5 invention 「創作」
7 the feminine scheme 「女性の衣装体系」
14 formally 「形の上で」
16 fabrics 「生地」
18 station in life 「身分」
21-for everything we have so far described 「これまで述べてきたすべてのものの」
24 display 「見世物」
two-sexed unit 「両性に合った単位」
24-a single visual illustration of 「～を示す一枚のイラスト」
26 at all levels of society 「社会の全階層に」
tinkers 「鋳掛け屋」
30 1 hasten to 「取り急ぎ～する」
2 say 「発言権」
results 「仕上がった服」
3 prestigious 「格式が高い」
5 man or woman 「顧客が男性であれ,女性であれ」

3. Later Changes

31 1 **Given the waywardness at the core of fashion** 「つむじまがりがファッションの中心にあるとすれば」
　　2–**disequilibrium** 「不安定」
　　4 **too easy** = very easy.
　　Contrary to folklore 「俗に考えられていることとは反対に」
　　9 **a defining element** 「〜の特徴を明らかにする決定的要素」
　　11 **problematic** 「不確実な」
　　12 **precarious** 「落ちてしまいそうな」
　　13–**remind...that 〜** 「...に〜を思い起こさせる」
　　privileged men and women 「特権階級の人々」
　　15 **elaborate** 「労を惜しまずに手間隙かけた」
　　16 **simple peons** 「無教育で社会身分の低い者たち」
　　18–**the comfort of such clothes was in the head** 「そうした衣装の快適さは，それを身に着けている人の頭の中にあった」

33 1 **social degree** 「社会身分」
　　3 **stale** 「生気を失った」
　　9 **reclarify the anatomical scheme** 「解剖学的体系を再び明瞭にする」
　　Neo-classic 「新古典主義の」 新古典主義は18世紀中期から19世紀中期にかけて発達。
　　10 **Baroque** 「バロック様式の」 バロック様式は，だいたい16世紀中期から18世紀中期に盛んであった複雑で華やかな建築・美術様式。
　　Rococo 「ロココ様式の」 18世紀中期のフランスの様式で，こみいった曲線模様と華やかな色彩をその特徴とする。
　　blurring 「ぼやけさせる」
　　14 **accident** 「偶然」
　　15 **perversity** 「つむじまがり」
　　17 **up to a point** 「ある程度は」
　　18–**proved itself obsolete in the field** 「戦場で用いられなくなった」
　　20 **vestigial** 「鎧かぶとの痕跡を残す」

33 20 **gorgets**　「喉当て」
　　　　breastplates　「胸当て」
　　21 **badges of rank**　「階級章」
　　　　the harrowing period　「悲惨な時代」
　　22 **the Thirty Years' War**　「30年戦争」　主としてドイツ国内における新旧両教徒のあいだの宗派戦争（1618-48）。
　　　　the English Civil War　ピューリタン革命のこと。チャールズ1世と議会の争い（1642-51）。
　　24 **the rough-and-ready soldier**　「にわか仕立ての兵士」
　　　　clad = clothed.
　　25 **jerkin**　「ジャーキン」　16世紀から17世紀の男子用の短い上着。
　　26 **bits and snatches**　「断片」
　　26-**showed through**　「顔をのぞかせた」
　　27 **flaps**　「垂れ」
　　　　slits　「スリット」,「切り込み」
34　1 **straps**　「肩帯」,「肩ひも」
　　2 **was accoutered with**　「～を身につけていた」
　　4 **To echo the flavor**　「このにわか兵士の着こなし方を反映させるために」
　　5 **affected swagger**　「肩で風を切るのを好んだ」
　　6 **sweeping cloaks**　「すそを引きずる外套」
　　7 **guard-room**　「詰め所」
　　8 **Van Dyck**　「ヴァン・ダイク」（1599-1641）フランドルの画家。英国王チャールズ1世の宮廷画家であった。
　　9 **Jacques Callot**　「ジャック・カロ」（1592-1635）フランスの彫版家・銅板画家。
　　10 **ruffs**　「ひだ襟」
　　　　clipped　「短く刈り込んだ」
　　　　footwear　「履き物」　Cf. *p.*23, *l.*20.
　　11-**orderly and imposing**　「規則正しく，堂々とした」
　　12 **containment**　「抑制」
　　13 **gave way to**　「～に取って代わられた」
　　14 **in harmony with**　「～と調子を合わせて」
　　15-**nonchalance**　「無頓着」

34 18 **open-collar** 「開襟」
　20 **flop** 「ゆれる」
　　 stubble 「ぶしょうひげ」
　22-**the gear of leisure moments** 「レジャー服」
　23 **dress wear** = formal wear.
　23-**The conscious, verbal justification of such moves** 「そうした動きへの意識的な理屈付け」
　25-**in the face of** 「〜をものともせずに」
　27 **abiding spirit of** 「〜という変わらない精神」
35 　2 **the iron demands** 「鉄のような強い要求」
　　3-**as severe about ease as it is [severe] about order**
　　6 **smooth shaving** 「ひげをはやさないこと」
　　7 **Given**　既出。Cf. *p*.31, *l*.1.
　　8 **instigation** 「そそのかし」
　11 **the prevailing flavor** 「流行している特色」
　13 **décolleté** 「えりぐりの大きい」　既出。
　　 deceptive 「人を迷わす」
　13-**shaping bodice** 「美しい身体を作るためのボディス」
　14 **goodly head** 「かなり大きい髪型」
　18 **rakish** 「自堕落な」
　22-**to which women have continued to help themselves** 「それを女性たちが自由に利用し続けた」
　24 **athletic** = of sports.
　26 **skin-divers** 「スキンダイバー」　アクアラングと足ヒレを使って潜水する人。
　27-**pit their bodily strength against huge odds** 「身体を使って大きな勝負に挑む」
36 　1 **takes note of** 「〜に注目する」
　　2 **extraterrestrials** = aliens. 「宇宙人」
　　2-**travellers into the future** 「未来への旅人」
　　3 **gamblers with the fate of the earth** 「地球の運命をかける者たち」
　　6 **molded plastic** 「成形プラスチック」
　　7 **sensational** 「大評判になる」
　　9 **Dandy mode** 「ダンディズム」

36　10　sporting　「スポーツに関した」
　　13-riding clothes　「乗馬服」
　　18　scope　「余地」
　　24　fancy dress　「仮装衣装」
　　25　until well on　「かなり～まで」
37　 6　Anomalous persons　「男装の麗人」　anomalous　「変態的な」
　　　　George Sand　既出。Cf. *p*.17, *l*.16.
　　　　Joan of Arc　既出。　Cf. *p*.23, *l*.10.
　　　7　in a virtual vacuum　「実質上外界と絶縁して」
　　　8　Amelia Bloomer　「アメリア・ブルーマー」(1818-94) アメリカの社会改革家。ブルーマーを創案する。
　　　9　came and went　「やってきて去った」
　　10　unseemly　「みっともない」
　　　　could only　「ただ～するしかなかった」
　　11-millennia　既出。Cf. *p*.27, *l*.17.
　　13　a layer of fabric　「一枚の服地」
　　14　figured　「登場した」
　　　　soft-core　「ソフトコアの」　性的露出がそれほどでない。
　　16　fast　「身持ちの悪い」
　　　　elegant society　「上流社会」
　　18　fisherfolk　「漁師」
　　20　"breeches" parts　「女優の演じる男役」
　　22　the Mysterious East　「神秘的な東洋」
　　22-which had its own dubious associations　「東洋それ自体にいかがわしい連想があった」
　　25　laggard　「ぐずぐずした」
38　 2　envelope　「包みこむ服」
　　 2-that formed a flattering modern commentary upon　「～についてうれしがらせるような現代的解釈をした」
　　 5　upholstering　「詰め物をして」
　　　　stiffening　「糊付けをして」
　　 7　skimmed　「～を滑って行った」
　　 7-in counterpoint to　「～の反対に」
　　 8-a mobile work of art　「動く芸術作品」

38 9 **combination** 「身体と衣服の組み合わせ」
   10 **was...pared down** 「削ぎ落とされた」
   11 **thinned** 「減少させられた」
   13 **careful** 「念の入った」
      formula 「一定の形式」
   15 **its actual composition** 「現実の肉体」
   18 **distracting** 「混乱させる」
   22 **acute** 「深刻な」
   23 **tailoring** 「仕立て」
   27 *sans-culotte* [sænzkjulát; *F* sãkylɔt] 「サンキュロット」「半ズボンなし」の意味のフランス語。フランス革命当時，貴族が下層階級の長ズボンをはいた共和党員を軽蔑してこう呼んだ。

39 1 **common sailors** 「下級船員」
    4 **plebeian connotations** 「庶民的な意味」
    4 **an undemanding loose alternative to** 「〜に代わる，きつくない，ゆったりとした衣服」
    5 **knee-breeches** 「ひざ丈のズボン」
    6 **skin-tight doeskin** 「体にぴったり合ったドースキンの」 ドースキンとは，雄鹿の革に似せて密に織った，光沢のあるラシャ織り。
    7 **had shown off** 「見せびらかした」
    8 **without much room for compromise** 「あまり妥協の余地なく」，「しっかりと」
   11 **and [were] assimilated**
   14 **answered harmoniously to** 「〜に調和した」
   15 **coat-skirts** 「上着の裾」 腰から下の部分。
   18 **phallic note** 「男根のしるし」
      basic ensemble 「基本的な上下服」
   19 **in place** 「整った」
   23 **civil leadership** 「文民指導者」
   25 **probity** 「誠実」,「廉直」
      detachment 「公平」
   26 **enlightened** 「すぐれた」
      seethe 「たぎる」

40 1 **more than a little menacing** 「少なからず威嚇的な」

40　1–its force [being] by no means spent
　　3　share the scene with suits　「スーツと共に見られる」
　　3–suits have shifted their posture　「スーツをめぐる状況は変わった」
　　5　self-esteem　「自尊心」

4. Female Invention

41　2　successive　「引き続く」
　　4　static　「つまらない」,「変化のない」
　　7　compelling effects　「強い影響」
　　　　trappings　「(装飾的)衣装」
　　10　Dürer　「デューラー」(1471–1528) ドイツ・ルネサンスの画家・版画家。
　　11　the male subjects　「男性の像」
　　　　Titian　「ティツィアーノ」(1487–1576) イタリア・ベネチア派画家。
　　12　Giorgione　「ジョルジョーネ」(1487–1511) イタリア・ベネチア派画家。
　　13　feminine cast　「女性らしさ」,「女性的特徴」
　　16　has little to do with　「～とほとんど関係がない」
　　17　ruthlessness　「残忍さ」
　　18　flavor　「趣」
42　3　close-fitting　「(身体に)密着する」
　　4　fall off　「落ちる」
　　8　clavicles　「鎖骨」
　　8–mercenaries　「傭兵」
　　10　foil　「引き立てるもの」
　　11　vigorously slashed　「大胆な裂け目を入れた」
　　12　a Humanist fashion　「人文主義的ファッション」　先行する"this vogue"の説明。
　　13–preoccupations　「関心」
　　16　it　次行の"the long loose hair"を指す。
　　19　Samson-style　「サムソンのスタイル」　Samsonはイスラエルの士師で、愛人Delilahに裏切られてペリシテ人に捕われ、盲目にさ

れるが，後に自らの命を犠牲にして復讐をとげる。旧約聖書の士師記 13－16 章に登場する。

42 21 **elaboration**「念入りな手入れ」
　22 **was braided, knotted up**「編まれ，結い上げられた」
　23 **trimmings**「飾り物」
　24 **the Virgin**「聖母マリア」
　25 **undressed**「手入れをしていない」
　　　when fashionably dressed up「正装しているときに」
　26 **-sexual reference**「性的意味」
　27 **-sensual susceptibility**「多情」

43　1 **standard**「広く知られている」
　1 **-Mary Magdalene**「マグダラのマリア」 新約聖書のルカ伝 7－8 章に登場する。
　2 **This is still the case in**「これは～にも依然としてあてはまる」
　4 **-a potent female attribute**「強力な女性の属性」
　5 **not correctly displayed in public**「礼儀正しくするためには人前で見せない」
　8 **cloak of hair**「髪のおおい」
　9 **field-lilies**「野の百合」
　10 **a kind of Edenic, surrogate nudity**「アダムとイブがエデンの園で汚れを知らずに裸でいたことの代りになるようなもの」
　11 **undissipated**「浪費されない」
　　　unadulterated「混ざり物のない」
　14 **brocade**「ブロケード」,「金襴」
　15 **both sexual and temporal**　前の power にかかる。「性的な力と世俗的な力」
　16 **Respectable matrons**「上品な既婚婦人」
　18 **ploy**「策略」
　　　domestic chastity「家庭内での貞節」
　23 **stature**「背丈」
　24 **in action**「元気に活動している」
　25 **modish** = fashionable.
　27 **conservative observers**「保守的な観察者」

44　1 **As is so often the case**「とてもよくあることだが」

44　3　**rubs off on**　「はがれて～にくっつく」
　　5-**free-swinging**　「無拘束の」
　　6-**count as another male borrowing**　「もう一つの男性からの借り物として見なされる」
　　15-**in this vein**　「この流れでの」
　　18　**in that vein**　「その流れで」
　　19　**midriff**　「胴の中間部」,「腹」
　　22　**bring...full circle**　「～を一巡させて元に戻す」
　　24　**that** = when.
　　26　**echo**　「～をそのまま真似る」
45　3　**tunics**　「チュニック」　スカートと合わせて着用する婦人用上着。
　　5　**initiative**　「主導」
　　8　**correct circumstances**　「正式の場」
　　8-**disturbing flavor**　「その場にそぐわない感じ」
　　12-**in negligent or hearty moods**　「だらしがないか，熱中している場合には」
　　13　**been moved to**　「～する気にさせられる」
　　19　**city wear** = street wear.　「外出着」
48　1-**of general masculine drapery**　前の survival にかかる。
　　2　**even for war**　「戦闘服としてさえ用いられた」
　　3　**coifs**　「(尼僧の) 頭巾」
　　6　**fitted**　「ぴったりする」
　　8　**cowls**　「(修道院の) 頭巾」
　　9　**plebeian**　「下層階級の」
　　10　**sweatshirts**　「(フードつきの) トレーナー」
　　20　**had finally made a clear link with**　「～とついに明確につながった」
　　21　**electrifying**　既出。Cf. *p*.27, *l*.15.
　　24-**upholstery**　「生地」
49　2　**vestigial**　「なごり程度の」
　　　　rib-cage　「胸部」
　　3　**elaborate**　「念入りに手をいれられた」
　　3-**took on...density**　「さらにこれまでよりも多種多様になり，大きくなり，幾重にも重ねたものになった」

49　6　**went to final extremes**　「最終的に極端になった」
　　9　**chrysalis**　「覆い」
　 10　**to include**　「〜を含むほどに」
　 12　**shrouded**　「覆われた」
　 13　**compelling**　「有力である」
　 14　**moments**　「時」
　 15　**has license to prevail**　「大手を振るえる」
　　　at the ball　「ダンスパーティで」
　 17　**It**　前の節の"The theme"を受ける。
　 19　**perniciously divided**　「致命的なほど上半身と下半身が分けられた」
　 23　**all that**　「そのようなものすべては」
　 24　**delicious**　「快い」
　 27　**Below, under the foam, the swirling waves** ＝ Under the foam and below the swirling waves.
　　　swirling　「渦巻く」
50　1　**shapeliness**　「形の良さ」
　　4　**enact their definitive escape**　「断固脱出する」
　　5　**Articulating**　「〜を明確にする」
　　9　**full humanity**　「完全な人間性」
　　9–**that meant showing that**　「それは〜ということを示すことであった」
　 10　**in many particulars**　「多くの点で」
　 11　**working legs**　「動く脚」
　 13　**tinselly**　「ぴかぴか光る」
　　　members　「手足」
　 14　**nether arms**　「地獄の腕」
　 15–**tendons**　「腱」
　 17　**by extension**　「そこから広がって」、「さらには」

図説部分

7　1　**bas-relief** [barilíːf]　「浅浮き彫り」
　　　elevation　「立面図」
　　2　**Byzantine**　「ビザンチン様式の」

7　2–*The Empress Theodora and Retinue*　「テオドラ皇后と従者たち」
　　3　**Ravenna**　「ラヴェンナ」　イタリア北東部の都市。
8　1　**Manuscript illumination**　「写本彩飾」
　　1–*Le Roman de la violette*　「スミレ物語」
　　3　**Master E.S.**　「巨匠 E.S.」　不詳。
32　1　**François Clouet**　「フランソワ・クルーエ」（1510–72）フランスの肖像画家。
　　1　*Le Duc d'Alençon*　「アランソン公爵」
　　2　**Sánchez Coello**　「サンチェス・コエリョ」　不詳。
46　1–*Henri II de Lorraine, duc de Guise*　「ギーズ公, アンリ・ド・ロレーヌ 2 世」
　　8　**crisply**　「くっきりと」
　　16　**coiffure** [kwa:fjúər]　「結髪」
　　19–**tactile**　「触覚の」
47　1　**Jan Vermeer**　「ヤン・フェルメール」（1632–75）オランダの画家。
　　3–**male references**　「男性服からの借り物」
　　8　**flaunt**　「誇示する」

性とスーツ
Sex and Suits

2001年1月20日　初版発行
2004年4月10日　第2刷発行

著　者　Anne Hollander
著　者　白井義昭
発行者　森　信久
発行所　株式会社　松柏社
　　　　〒102-0072　東京都千代田区飯田橋1-6-1
　　　　TEL 03 (3230) 4813（代表）
　　　　FAX 03 (3230) 4857
　　　　e-mail: shohaku@ss.iij4u.or.jp

表紙イラスト　　安藤千種（パラダイス・ガーデン）
表紙デザイン　　ローテリニエ・スタジオ
製版・印刷・製本　モリモト印刷（株）
ISBN4-88198-494-2
略号＝494

Copyright on Notes © 2001 by Yoshiaki Shirai

本書を無断で複写・複製することを禁じます。
落丁・乱丁は送料小社負担にてお取り替え致します。

📼 本書にはカセットテープがございます。